P9-CDB-800

3

Rookie Read-About® Holidays

Kwanzaa

by Lisa M. Herrington

Content Consultants

Nanci R. Vargus, Ed.D.
Professor Emeritus, University of Indianapolis

Carrie A. Bell, MST Visual Arts – All Grades
Julia A. Stark Elementary School, Stamford, Connecticut

Reading Consultant

Jeanne M. Clidas, Ph.D.
Reading Specialist

Children's Press®
An Imprint of Scholastic Inc.
New York Toronto London Auckland Sydney
Mexico City New Delhi Hong Kong
Danbury, Connecticut

Library of Congress Cataloging-in-Publication Data
Herrington, Lisa M.
  Kwanzaa / by Lisa M. Herrington.
    pages cm. — (Rookie read-about holidays)
  Includes index.
  ISBN 978-0-531-27204-6 (library binding) — ISBN 978-0-531-27354-8 (pbk.)
  1. Kwanzaa—Juvenile literature. I. Title.
  GT4403.H47 2013
  394.2612—dc23   2013014854

Produced by Spooky Cheetah Press

© 2014 by Scholastic Inc.

All rights reserved. Published in 2014 by Children's Press, an imprint of Scholastic Inc.

Printed in China 62

SCHOLASTIC, CHILDREN'S PRESS, ROOKIE READ-ABOUT®, and associated logos
are trademarks and/or registered trademarks of Scholastic Inc.

1 2 3 4 5 6 7 8 9 10 R 23 22 21 20 19 18 17 16 15 14

Photographs © 2014: Adam Chinitz: 28; age fotostock/John Burke: 4, 31 bottom;
AP Images/Ken Ruinard/Anderson Independent-Mail: 8; Getty Images: 12, 31
center top (Bill O'Leary/The Washington Post), cover (Burke/Triolo Productions),
20 (Robert Abbott Sengstacke); Keith Plechaty: 11, 30; Louise Gardner: 6; Media
Bakery: 27 (Blend Images), 19 (Hill Street Studios), 16, 31 center bottom (Stockbyte);
Science Source/Lawrence Migdale: 24; Superstock, Inc./Belinda Images: 15; The
Image Works/E.A. Kennedy: 23, 31 top; Thinkstock: 3 bottom (Comstock), 3 top
(iStockphoto).

Table of Contents

Happy Kwanzaa!

It is time to celebrate! Kwanzaa (KWAHN-zah) is a holiday that honors African-American **culture** and life today.

Kwanzaa is a time for families to gather together.

5

Kwanzaa is a week-long celebration at the end of the year.

Kwanzaa lasts for seven days, from December 26th to January 1st. Families gather together. They eat African food, share stories, and give gifts.

FAST FACT!

Kwanzaa comes from an African word. It stands for the first fruits picked at the **harvest**.

6

DECEMBER

SUNDAY	MONDAY	TUESDAY	WEDNESDAY	THURSDAY	FRIDAY	SATURDAY
	1	2	3	4	5	6
7	8	9	10	11	12	13
14	15	16	17	18	19	20
21	22	23	24	25	26	27
28	29	30	31	1 January	2	3

7

How It Began

Kwanzaa began in the United States in 1966. An African-American teacher named Maulana Karenga started it. He wanted people to learn about their past in Africa.

Maulana Karenga is a professor of African studies.

9

Seven ideas are at the heart of Kwanzaa. People try to live by these ideas. Each one is celebrated on a different day of Kwanzaa.

Seven Ideas of Kwanzaa

Day	Idea
Day 1: December 26	**Umoja** (oo-MOH-jah): unity; standing together
Day 2: December 27	**Kujichagulia** (koo-jee-cha-goo-LEE-ah): being true to yourself
Day 3: December 28	**Ujima** (oo-JEE-mah): working together
Day 4: December 29	**Ujamaa** (oo-jah-MAH): sharing
Day 5: December 30	**Nia** (NEE-ah): having a purpose or goal
Day 6: December 31	**Kuumba** (koo-OOM-bah): creating something
Day 7: January 1	**Imani** (ee-MAH-nee): faith in yourself and your community

Kwanzaa's Symbols

Families decorate their homes in red, black, and green. Black stands for the African-American people. Red stands for their struggles. Green stands for hope.

The Kwanzaa flag, shown at upper left, is called a bendera.

13

To get ready for Kwanzaa, people gather seven **symbols**. The symbols are a mat, corn, fruits and vegetables, a candleholder, seven candles, a cup, and gifts.

This photo shows a girl and her grandmother with Kwanzaa symbols.

14

The mat is called the mkeka (em-KAY-kah). It stands for the African past. People place other Kwanzaa symbols on the mat.

A mkeka may be made of straw or other materials.

17

People put one ear of corn for each child in their family on the mat. They place fruits and other vegetables on the mat. These are symbols of the harvest. They are called mazao (mah-ZAH-oh).

This man will place three ears of corn—one for each child—on the mat.

The kinara (kee-NAR-uh) is a wooden candleholder. It holds seven candles—three red, one black, and three green. Families light one candle each night. The black candle is lit on the first night.

FUN FACT!

The kinara stands for people who lived in Africa long ago. The seven candles stand for Kwanzaa's seven ideas.

Spreading Joy

To celebrate Kwanzaa, families sing, dance, and play music. Some people dress in colorful African clothing.

These young girls are performing a traditional African dance.

22

Families enjoy meals together during Kwanzaa. They also drink from a special cup called a **unity** cup. It is a symbol of staying together. A big feast is held on December 31.

The Kwanzaa feast includes traditional African and Southern foods.

On the last day of Kwanzaa, people give homemade gifts called zawadi (zah-WAH-dee). They might include a beaded bracelet and a book of African stories. The gifts reward kids for promises kept during the year. Have *you* kept your promises this year?

Kwanzaa gifts are given to children who have behaved well during the year.

Make a Kwanzaa Hat

28

What You'll Need

- White construction paper
- Scissors
- Stapler
- Index card
- Black, red, and green crayons or markers
- Glue stick

Directions

1. With an adult's help, cut two strips of white paper to make long rectangles that are each 3 inches wide. Ask the adult to staple the ends of the rectangles together to make one long rectangle. Then ask him or her to measure the long rectangle around your head and cut off the excess paper.

2. Use the crayons and the index card to make a red, black, and green Kwanzaa flag. Glue the flag to the center of the long strip. This will be the front of your hat.

3. Use the crayons to add other Kwanzaa decorations to your hat, such as a unity cup, ears of corn, and small gifts.

4. Ask an adult to wrap the hat around your head and staple the ends of the strip to fit.

Show What You Know!

Kwanzaa's Special Ideas

Use the chart to answer these questions.

- On which day of Kwanzaa do some families work together on a chore? What chore could your family do together?

- On which day of Kwanzaa do kids think about what they want to be when they grow up? What do you want to be? Why?

Seven Ideas of Kwanzaa

Day	Idea
Day 1: December 26	**Umoja** (oo-MOH-jah): unity; standing together
Day 2: December 27	**Kujichagulia** (koo-jee-cha-goo-LEE-ah): being true to yourself
Day 3: December 28	**Ujima** (oo-JEE-mah): working together
Day 4: December 29	**Ujamaa** (oo-jah-MAH): sharing
Day 5: December 30	**Nia** (NEE-ah): having a purpose or goal
Day 6: December 31	**Kuumba** (koo-OOM-bah): creating something
Day 7: January 1	**Imani** (ee-MAH-nee): faith in yourself and your community

A Celebration of Seven

The number seven has important meaning during Kwanzaa. Go back through the book and find three examples of how the number seven is worked into the holiday.

Glossary

culture (KUHL-chur): the way of life, ideas, customs, and traditions of a group of people

harvest (HAR-vist): the gathering of crops that are ripe

symbols (SIM-buhls): things that stand for something else

unity (YOO-nih-tee): togetherness

Index

Facts for Now

Visit this Scholastic Web site for more information on Kwanzaa:
www.factsfornow.scholastic.com
Enter the keyword **Kwanzaa**

About the Author

Lisa M. Herrington is a freelance writer and editor. She especially loves writing for children. Lisa lives in Trumbull, Connecticut, with her husband, Ryan, and her daughter, Caroline.